This sheet music contains two arrangements of the theme from Disney-Pixar's movie _UP_. Both versions are basically the same, except for the range of strings used. The first arrangement is for pedal harp and most lever harps. The range goes from the G that is about 1½ octaves below middle C, up to the G that is about 2½ octaves above middle C. The second arrangement is for small harps with only one octave below middle C. Additional instructions are provided with both arrangements advising you on what to do if your harp does not include the highest G needed.

If you play a lever harp, be sure to set your levers as indicated before you begin. Lever changes within the piece are indicated by diamond notes, and also in words between the treble and bass clef staves. "High C" is the C that is one octave above middle C, and "very high C" is 2 octaves above middle C.

Pedal harpists should set their pedals for the key signature. Pedal changes are written below the bass clef staff.

Thank you for purchasing this music. I hope you enjoy playing this sweet, tender piece.

Sylvia Woods

With special thanks to Paul Baker and Jonathan Heely

Harp arrangements © 2009 by Sylvia Woods, Woods Music & Books, Inc.

Published by Woods Music & Books, Inc.
P.O. Box 816, Montrose CA 91021, U.S.A.

www.harpcenter.com

ISBN 978-0-936661-53-7

1

Up
Theme from Disney-Pixar's Up
arranged for pedal harp
and lever harps with 10 or more strings below middle C

Lever harp players: set middle C# in
addition to the F#s before you begin.

The highest note in this piece is the G that is 2½ octaves above middle C.
If your harp does not go this high, see the instructions on the bottom of page 3.

Music by Michael Giacchino
Harp arrangement by Sylvia Woods

Moderately and expressively

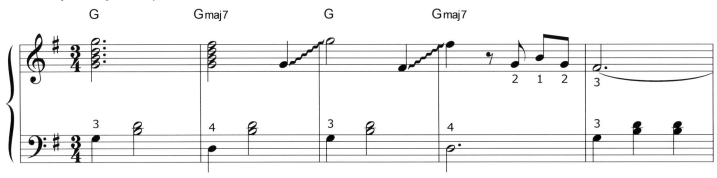

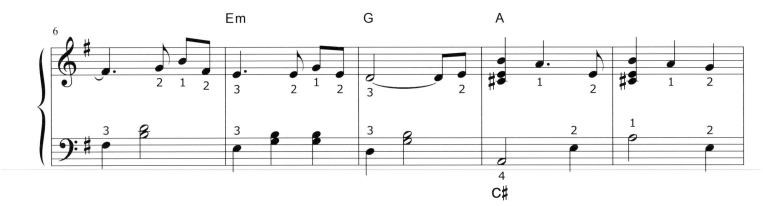

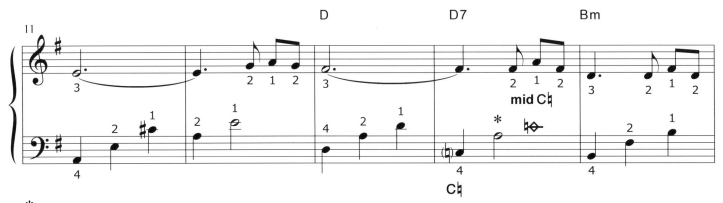

* Lever harp players may play the 2nd bass clef beat of measure 14 with the right hand to facilitate the lever change.

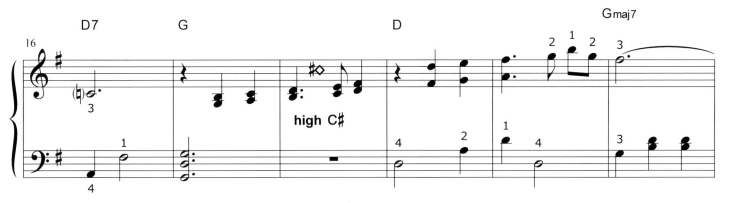

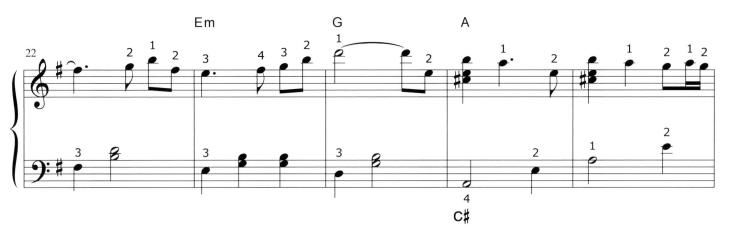

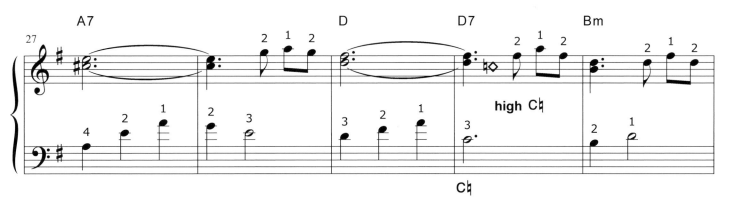

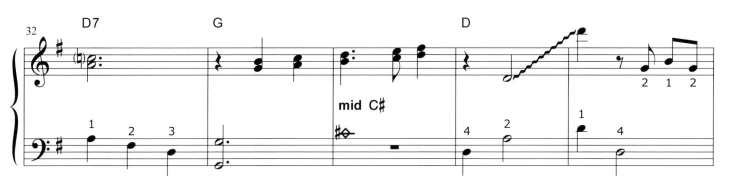

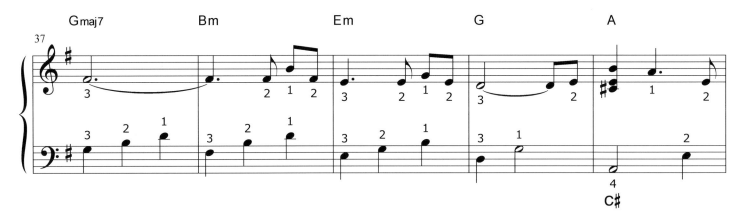

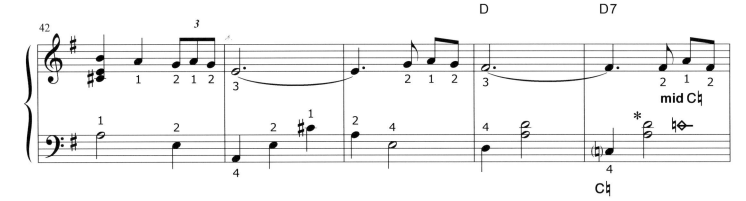

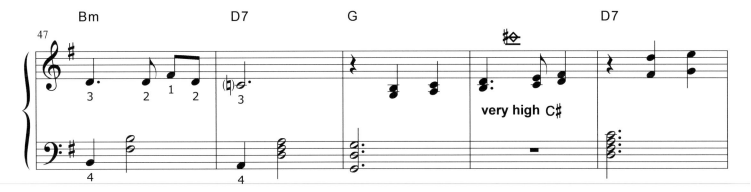

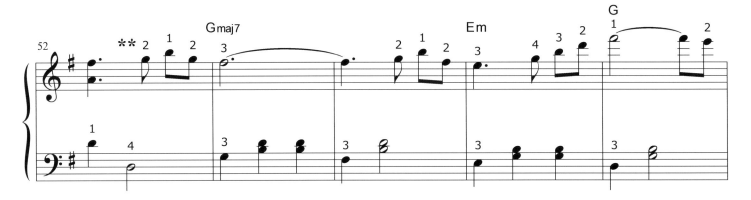

* Lever harp players may play the 2nd bass clef beat of measure 46 with the right hand to facilitate the lever change.

** If your harp does not have enough high strings for this section, play the right hand an octave lower through the middle of measure 60. You will need to add a high C# lever change in measure 56, and change back to natural at the end of measure 60.

4

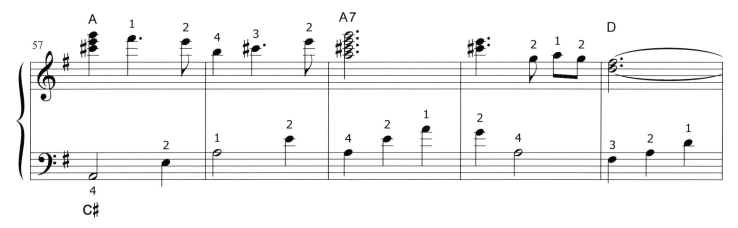

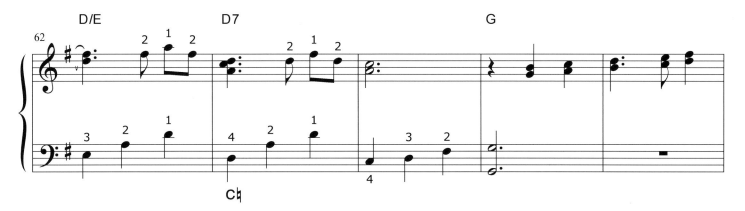

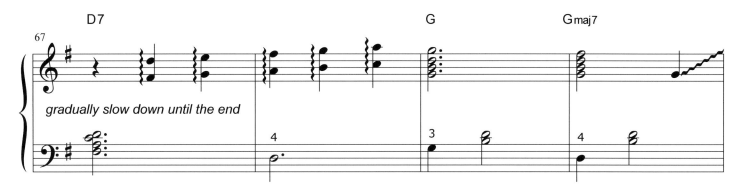

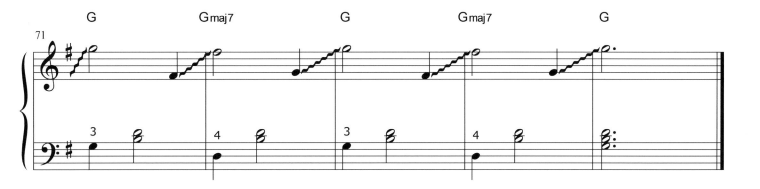

Up
Theme from Disney-Pixar's *Up*
arranged for small harps with 1 octave below middle C

Music by Michael Giacchino
Harp arrangement by Sylvia Woods

Lever harp players: set middle C# and very high C#
in addition to the F#s before you begin.

The highest note in this piece is the G that is 2½ octaves above middle C.
If your harp does not go this high, see the instructions on the bottom of page 7.

Moderately and expressively

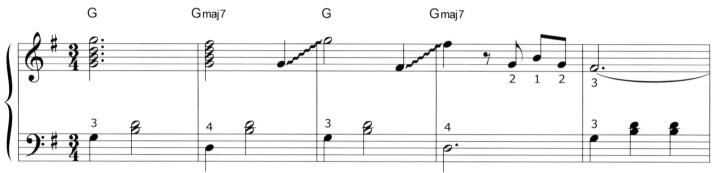

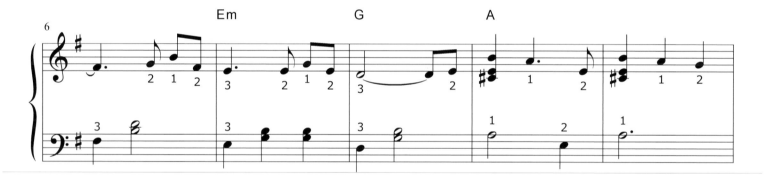

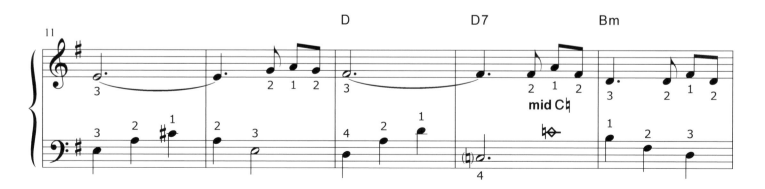

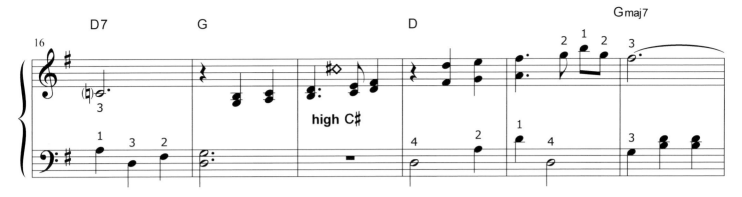

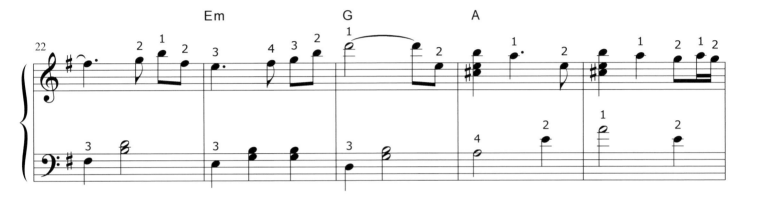

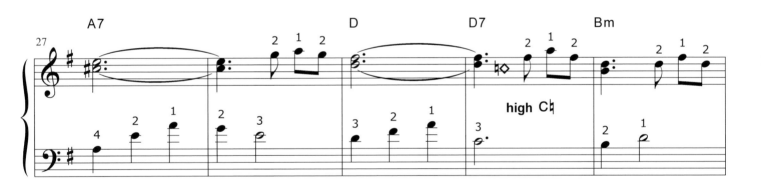

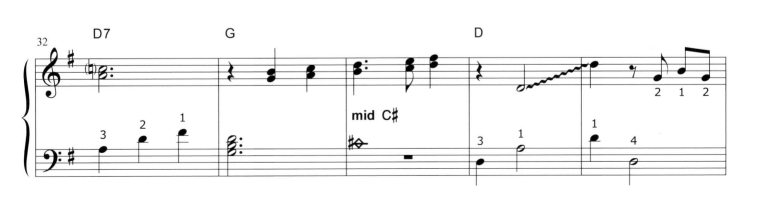

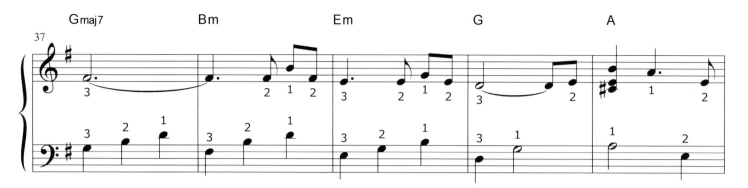

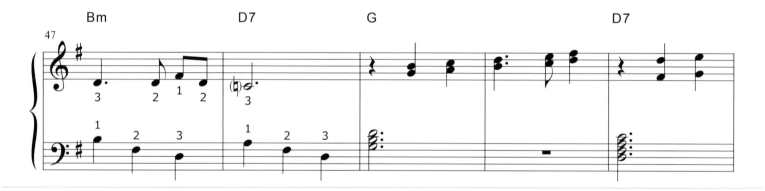

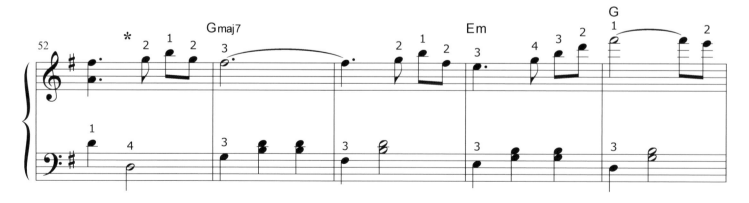

* If your harp does not have enough high strings for this section, play the right hand an octave lower through the middle of measure 60. You will need to add a high C# lever change in measure 56, and change back to natural at the end of measure 60.